NEW
WELSH READER

New Welsh Reader
New Welsh Review Ltd
PO Box 170, Aberystwyth, SY23 1WZ
Telephone: 01970 628410
www.newwelshreview.com

Editor: Gwen Davies
editor@newwelshreview.com

Administration & Finance Officer:
Bronwen Williams
admin@newwelshreview.com

Marketing & Publicity Officer:
Edie Franklin
marketing@newwelshreview.com

Management Board:
Ali Anwar, Gwen Davies (Director),
Andrew Green (Director, Chair), Ruth
Killick, David Michael (Treasurer),
Matthew Francis, Emily Blewitt (Poetry
Subs Editor, Vice-Chair)

Aberystwyth University Partnership:
TK Quentin

**Sponsor of the New Welsh Writing
Awards:** RS Powell

Design: Ingleby Davies Design
Host: Aberystwyth University

Main images: Front cover photograph
of Jan Morris © MR Thomas; contents
page, front inside cover & back cover
photographs: Vanessa Winship (from
Snow, Deadbeat Club, 2022).

With special thanks to Creative Wales (a
Welsh Government initiative) for a Cost-
of-Living Emergency Fund.

The New Welsh Review Ltd publishes with
the financial support of the Books Council
of Wales, and is hosted by Aberystwyth
University's Department of English &
Creative Writing. The New Welsh Review
Ltd was established in 1988 by Academi
(now Literature Wales) and the Association
for Welsh Writing in English. *New Welsh
Reader* is New Welsh Review's print (and
digital) magazine for creative work. We
also publish monthly roundups of online
content, including reviews, comment and
poetry, and at least one book annually on
the New Welsh Rarebyte imprint, run a
writing competition (New Welsh Writing
Awards), and improve diversity in the UK
publishing industry by hosting student work
placements.

Mae croeso ichi ohebu â'r golygydd
yn Gymraeg.

Patrons: Belinda Humfrey, Owen Sheers

Ariennir gan
Lywodraeth Cymru
Funded by
Welsh Government

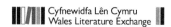

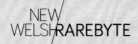

SIGN UP!

Our new website can be browsed by category, theme tag or title and is now a one-stop shop for our ePub formats and fully searchable digital archive, books, offers & more. New-look digital editions are fully searchable, have page-turning feature and include complete text to speech (TTS) element as standard.

newwelshreview.com

NEW WELSH REVIEW

REVIEWS, COMMENT, POETRY

Poems on dogs and love by Kevin Cahill, on knitting and fishing by Jessica Mayhew, and on maternity by KS Moore

Travel book roundup trekking from Tibet to Hay-on-Wye with Chris Moss and Rhiannon Hooson

Demtso of Dong Tsang clan at nomad camp, Lalung Valley, Nangchen, Kham, 2014.

© DIANE BARKER, FROM PORTRAITS OF TIBET

Memoir review *Delicacy: A Memoir about Cake and Death* Ed Garland gobbles up this rigorous, crafted and very funny exploration of the links between cake and human distress by the Welsh comedian and *Ghosts* actor

Nonfiction review *Night Terrors: Troubled Sleep and the Stories We Tell about It* Leah Larwood is fascinated by a nonfiction title that confronts the author's own strange and frightening night-time encounters, and the scientific and cultural backdrop of sleep disorders

Reportage Ellen Bell is part-way through her year-long reportage residency at Ruthin Craft Centre, Ruthin and Oriel Davies, Newtown, in which her listening and storytelling skills, 'a Barbara Pym kind of drawn narrative', are as important as her drawing skills

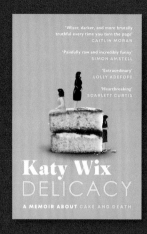

'Wiser, darker, and more brutally truthful every time you turn the page'
CAITLIN MORAN

'Painfully raw and incredibly funny'
SIMON AMSTELL

'Extraordinary'
LOLLY ADEFOPE

'Heartbreaking'
SCARLETT CURTIS

Katy Wix
DELICACY
A MEMOIR ABOUT CAKE AND DEATH

From Ruthin Craft Centre residency, Helen Yardley rug in background, 2022.

© ELLEN BELL

NEW WELSH/READER

#133 ESSAYS, MEMOIR, STORIES, POETRY

Winners of the New Welsh Writing Awards 2023

NEW WELSH/WRITING AWARDS 2023

ICE

STORY BY **JEM POSTER**

PHOTOGRAPHS BY **VANESSA WINSHIP**

As I drive out of town the wind is rising, whipping the powdery snow from the roadside shrubs and sending it whirling across the black-top. I know what I'm looking for but I see the sign a moment too late. The surface is treacherous. I let the car slow to walking pace before I brake.

I reverse carefully and draw up level with the turning, a rutted track shadowed by conifers. The signboard hangs on two chains from a crude wooden frame. *Brody, sculptor* – just that, the letters bleached and peeling. I hear the chains creak as the wind catches the board.

The frozen grasses brush the underbody as I drive up the track. A flicker of anxiety – what if I ground the car out here, if I can't get it back to the road? – and then the track veers left and opens out on to a paved yard.

On the far side of the yard a long, low building. Rough board walls, sheet metal roof, the remains of a porch framing the door. Nailed to the boards, in the space between two of the windows, a tattered Confederate flag; above it a carved wooden eagle with its tail fanned and its wings outspread. A battered pickup is parked with its nose to the wall. I pull in alongside it, grab my camera bag and get out.

No sound but the wind. The snow around the doorway unprinted. If it wasn't for the smoke pluming from the stovepipe I'd think the place was deserted. I look out beyond the building to the piled clouds edged with sunlight and feel the old thrill – the vertiginous sense of possibility as I step away from my own life and close in on someone else's.

The door opens. I can just make out the man's bulk in the shadows. For a moment he hangs back, looking out, and then he steps forward to the threshold.

He's perfect. I visualise his gaunt, creased face lit from the side – natural light if I can set things up before it fades. He'll be hunched over his work, his lank hair falling forward, his hands guiding the tool. It's all there in my mind's eye, down to the thin flake of wood curling off the blade.

'Mr Brody?'

'Brody. Just Brody. What do you want?'

'I'm Anna. Anna Markham. I'm a photographer. I wonder if you'd be willing to let me sit in on your work for an hour or so. I just want a few shots. I won't be in your way.'

'I'm not working today.' He leans against the door-jamb, folds his arms across his chest. 'Who sent you?'

'The receptionist at the motel gave me your name. Told me where to find you.'

'I don't mean that. I mean who's this for? A newspaper?'

'It's a commission from a publisher. There'll be a book, a London exhibition. Maybe a show in New York if my agent can pull it off.'

'You're famous?'

He steps out into the yard, closing the door behind him. I've got his interest now.

'People in the business know my name. My work sells. If that's fame, I'm famous.'

'You live in London?'

'Cardiff.'

He frowns. I can see he has no idea. 'Wales,' I tell him. 'Cardiff's the capital.'

'And you've come all the way over to Fulton County just to photograph me?'

'You and others. The publisher wants a series of portraits showing people at work. People who still practise the old rural crafts.'

He fixes me with a hard stare. 'Rural crafts? You're going to hang me on a wall with a bunch of carpenters and quilt-stitchers? You saw the signboard. Sculptor. I'm an artist, lady, not a craftsman.'

I'm not about to debate the matter. I want that sidelit shot. 'You'll be in good company,' I say.

He reaches for the handle, opens the door. His eyes are still fixed on mine. I step forward, thinking he's going to invite me in, but he shakes his head. 'I'm sorry,' he says. 'You've come a long way for nothing.'

I'm not done yet. I know how to talk my way into people's homes, into their lives. And out again when the time comes. I give him my brightest smile.

'London,' I say. 'New York. Your portrait on display. Think about it.'

I can see him weighing it up. 'You'll tell them who I am?'

'I don't know who you are. Not yet. Give me an hour of your time and maybe I'll have some idea.'

'You know what I'm saying. Will my name be up there with the picture?'

'I'll make sure it is.'

'You'll say I'm a sculptor?'

'If it matters to you.'

He thrusts his hand into his trouser pocket and pulls out a clutch of keys. 'I'll show you,' he says. He leads me round to the side of the building.

From this angle the place looks more like a barn than a dwelling. Double doors, a doorway large enough to admit a horse and cart. He unlocks the right-hand door, grips the handle and pulls. The door sticks on the frozen snow. He tugs and scuffs until there's an opening wide enough for us to pass through.

A showroom, the motel receptionist told me, and I suppose this must be it, though she was obviously stretching a point. A wide, raftered space lit by a row of disproportionately large windows running the length of the back wall. Hard up against the wall a workbench, tools scattered anyhow across its surface. Barked sections of tree-trunk standing upright like sentinels; the floor littered with chips and shavings. There's only one item on show, a massive figure of a hawk. Brody leads me towards it.

The detail is remarkable, each feather sharply defined, but there's a stiffness about the piece, a symmetry more heraldic than lifelike. The bird sits on a plinth carved to represent weathered rock, its wings held out a little from its body. Superficially striking, I think, but not the work of an artist; and then I catch sight of a detail in the wings' shadow, a rabbit clasped in one of the bird's scaled talons.

I bend forward for a closer look. This is something different. The rabbit's body appears soft and pliable, the slack droop of the neck and shoulders following the contours of the rock. Where the talons grip the haunches, the fur is dinted; I imagine the flesh pierced to the bone. An odd paradox: in this small, finely realised death Brody has caught the life missing from the figure rearing above it.

He has come up close behind me – a little too close. I edge away. 'You know how long it takes me to make a piece like this?' he asks.

'Tell me.'

'Two, three months. And you know how much I'll get for it? A thousand, if I'm lucky. My wife used to say I was crazy, spending so much time for so little, but it's not just about the money, is it? You remember the parable of the talents? If you've got the gift it's a sin not to use it. That's what the Bible tells us and that's what I believe, but it wouldn't hurt to have the money too. And I could if I wasn't stuck in the boondocks. Put this in a New York gallery and it'll fetch ten times what anyone will pay me out here.'

My silence lasts a little too long, but he doesn't seem to notice. 'The rabbit,' I say at last. 'That's really something.'

He dips into his shirt pocket and brings out a dog-eared visiting card. 'Here's an idea,' he says. He holds the card towards me. 'I've got a stack of these in the house. I'll give them to you when you go. You can take them to the gallery – maybe set them on a shelf alongside the picture.'

'I don't think that would be possible.'

'Then put them anywhere they'll be seen, anywhere they can be picked up. Picked up by city folk, gallery folk. That way they can track me down.'

'Track you down?'

'When they see my work they'll want to know how to get hold of it.'

I need to set him straight. 'The photograph,' I say carefully, 'would be a portrait showing you working at your bench. You'll be the subject, not your work.'

He lays a hand on the hawk's rump. 'Suppose I pretend to be putting the finishing touches to this,' he says. 'Then you stand back, over there by the window, and you can have it all in one shot – me and my work together.'

I don't like pretence, and I don't let my subjects dictate terms. 'Let me take the shots I want,' I say. 'Then I'll take the shots you want. You can use them as you like.'

'But they won't be on view in the gallery?'

'That wouldn't be appropriate.'

His eyes narrow. 'Seems to me,' he says sharply, 'this is a one-sided deal. It's all you, isn't it? – you turning up on my doorstep, wanting my time, wanting a piece of me for your show. How about you give me something in return?'

There's a dull flush on his face and neck. I glance towards the doorway, suddenly uneasy. He must have caught the movement. When he speaks again the edge has gone from his voice.

'Listen,' he says, 'all I want is a little respect for my art. You've had your breaks or you wouldn't be where you are now. Why not give something back? Why not help me?'

I could tell him it doesn't happen like that. I could tell him there'd be no interest in his kind of work in any of the circles I move in. I could tell him I'm not particularly interested myself. I won't, of course. I need to get things back on track.

'I'll do what I can,' I say. 'But we'd better get moving.' I set my camera bag down on the floor and squat to unzip it. 'Before the light goes.'

I look up at him over my shoulder. It's obvious he's not listening. 'There's another piece,' he says. 'In the house. You need to see it.' He starts towards the doorway.

'Let's do this first. If there's time afterwards I'll take a look.'

'That's the wrong way round. Without seeing this you can't know who I am, you can't know whose picture you're taking. You'll find it's worth your time.'

I glance at the windows, gauging the light. 'Just five minutes,' I say, rising. 'Then the photographs.'

I shoulder my bag again. He leads the way back out into the yard and round to the front door.

A whiff of stale food and damp cloth as we enter. I look around the room, trying to get a sense of the man. Not much to go on: a worn sofa, four wooden chairs, a bookcase housing a collection of paperbacks; on a rough pine table a greasy plate and a clutter of stained mugs.

He must know what I'm thinking. 'My wife passed three years ago,' he says. 'She kept it nice. Say what you like, a man needs a woman about the house.' He leans in, slips the camera bag from my shoulder and hooks it over the back of the nearest chair.

'This way.' He leads me further in, stops in front of a narrow doorway.

'This was her room. After she took sick.' He pushes back the door. 'It's still her room, come to that.'

Against the far wall an iron bedstead draped with a patchwork coverlet, a rocking-chair at its foot. The curtains are half drawn so the light is muted. It's obvious he wants me to enter but I hang back.

'Go on in,' he says. 'She won't mind.'

The figure startles me. It stands against the wall, just inside the room, life-size or a little more, a naked woman reaching upward so her raised hand almost touches the ceiling. There's the same attention to detail – the delicate features, the tumble of curls mantling the neck and shoulders, the scrub of pubic hair, the nails of the toes and fingers – but otherwise this piece bears no relation to the figure of the hawk. This is energy embodied, caught in the lift of the feet from the plinth they stand on, in the stretch of the torso, the upward tilt of the head and the yearning reach of the right hand for something invisibly beyond its grasp.

Brody is watching me. 'You like her?' he asks.

Something in the figure has brought me to the verge of tears. I nod, not trusting my voice.

'There's not a day goes by,' he says, 'that I don't think of her.' He places his palm against the hollow of her back. 'I carved this in the months after she died. I was in a kind of fever, half crazy with grief. I couldn't rest. I'd be working past midnight, then up again before dawn, trying to find the shape and feel of her, trying to keep her by me.' He slides his hand down over the smooth grain of her hip, a lover's gesture, unsettlingly intimate. 'And there's something of her in the piece, no doubt about it. Something of myself too – the want in me, the ache I can't shuck off.'

I can tell he wants to talk, but there's no time for that. I make to leave the room but he's blocking the doorway and doesn't move aside. 'We need to be quick,' I say, 'or we'll lose the light.'

A long pause. I hear the stovepipe whistling in the wind. 'If you want,' he says at last, 'you could stay over. Sleep here. That way there's no rush. You can take your pictures tomorrow morning.'

'I'm afraid my schedule isn't flexible.' The brush-off is meant to sound businesslike but my voice is thin and unsteady.

'You'd be back on the road by ten. It's no problem to me – won't take me two minutes to make up the bed.'

Still he doesn't move. I feel my chest tighten. 'Tell you what,' I say, determinedly casual, 'I'll think it over while you make us a coffee. How does that sound?'

'There's only instant. Will that do?'

I relax a little. 'That'll be fine.' He ducks out of the doorway, letting me through. He gathers the dirty mugs from the table and carries them away into a side-room. I hear the kettle filling, the dull clank as he sets it down. I pick up my bag and make for the front door.

The car starts first time but he must have heard me leave the house because as I reverse out of the yard he's already there, framed in the doorway, stretching out his arms as if to draw me back. I catch a glimpse of his face and see, or imagine I see, the hurt in his eyes; his lips are moving but the words are lost on the wind. It crosses my mind that I've wronged him, that I'm letting him down in some way, but I shove the thought aside, swing away and accelerate down the track [story continues on p24].

ICE

[story continued from p14] Once I'm on the road I settle back in my seat and let out a long breath. The sun, dipping towards the horizon, breaks suddenly through a rift in the cloud, touching twigs and branches with fire, glancing off the windows of a derelict factory, off the iced surface of a flooded field. Ten seconds, twenty at most, before the landscape dims again, but the vision has lifted me. I drive on towards the town with a sense of purpose. I want a shower, I want a meal, I want to forget my wasted afternoon.

The deer seems to come out of nowhere, a brown blur in the failing light, moving at speed across my path. I hear a faint thud as I brake; then I feel the tail of the car slew round and I'm drifting, side on, down the road. I'm grappling with the steering wheel, pulling back on it crazily, as though that might bring the long, helpless slide to an end, but it's not until the wheels hit the verge that the car slows and comes to a juddering stop. I turn off the engine, scramble out and look back up the road.

I can see the deer, dark against the snow on the roadside bank. It's standing, but as I approach it moves further up the slope, walking with a strange hobbling gait, and I know that I've hit it. There's nothing I can do. It limps on and melts into the shadows beneath a stand of firs.

I hurry back to the car. I'm desperate to be off, but I'm shaking so badly that I don't trust myself to drive. I sit there with my hands gripping the wheel and take deep shuddering breaths, trying to calm myself. After a while I start to cry, quietly at first and then with abandon, throwing my head back and howling like a child. Crying for the deer, I suppose, maimed and doubtless doomed, and for the lonely man reaching out from his doorway for whatever it is he wants and can't have. And perhaps also for myself, a restless wanderer catching at the lives of others while my own life slips from my grasp.

I need to get moving. I set my lips tight and brush away the tears with the back of my hand. I half turn, fumbling for the seatbelt, and see the glare of headlights on the road behind me. As the vehicle draws near it slows, then swerves and pulls in a little ahead of me. An ancient pickup with only one working brake-light.

Brody? Could be anyone. The brake-light goes off, the door swings wide. I reach for the ignition. The driver hauls himself out into the buffeting wind and straightens up. My fingers close on the key, but I don't turn it. I lean forward, peering through the clouded windscreen and the gathering dusk, trying to make out who he is, waiting to see what he wants.

Vanessa Winship is an award-winning photographer (two World Press Photo prizes, 1998 and 2008; Sony World Photographer of the Year, 2008; and the Henri Cartier Bresson Award, 2011). Her work is held in many collections, including the National Portrait Gallery, the Sir Elton John collection, the Henri Cartier Bresson Foundation and Tate Britain. Her photographic monographs include *Schwarzes Meer* (2007), *Sweet Nothings* (2008), *she dances on Jackson* (2013), *And Time Folds* (2018), *Sète#19* (2019) and *Seeing the Light of Day* (2020). The photographs published here are a selection from her most recent monograph, *Snow* (published by Deadbeat Club, 2022), a collaboration with Jem Poster that interleaves images of rural Ohio and the Amish community with the answering short story, 'Ice'. vanessawinship.com

Jem Poster is the author of two novels, *Courting Shadows* (Sceptre, 2002) and *Rifling Paradise* (Sceptre, 2006), as well as a collection of poetry, *Brought to Light* (Bloodaxe, 2001). He is editor of Volume III in the six-volume *Edward Thomas: Prose Writings* (Oxford University Press, 2018) and co-author, with Sarah Burton, of a handbook for fiction writers, *The Book You Need to Read to Write the Book You Want to Write* (Cambridge University Press, 2022). The online courses he runs with Sarah Burton for writers of all levels can be found at https://between-the-lines-9bdd51.webflow.io

ALL THE WORLD IN A WELSH HAYLOFT

WHEN **MR THOMAS**
MET JAN MORRIS

PHOTOS © MR THOMAS

SHE WAS WAITING FOR ME AT THE ENTRANCE TO THE VILLAGE, LEANT UP against a dusty old Honda and fumbling with large oval beads that hung like regalia over a yellow knit jersey. She wore a look of sequestered contentment. Her mouth was puckered into a silent whistle and her eyebrows tapered thoughtfully into toppling white curls that soon came billowing across the concrete plain between us. Jan Morris was all of eighty, and luminous as a daffodil.

'Yes, yes, I know, it's the ugliest car park in Europe,' she said by way of a greeting, 'but finding the house can be tricky if you've not been before.' She cupped her eyes, pressed her face to my car window and began to scan the interior. The world's great urban wanderer had always obeyed a precept from the Psalms to 'grin like a dog and run about through the city', but a car's contents, its dashboard litter and stickered adornments, could give you the shape of a place just as well.

'Hop in,' she said, and with a jolt we took off through Llanystumdwy, past the glinting Dwyfor and the old goat's stone bright with moss, to a turning that left behind the wider Wales for a buff beaten track enfolded by twisted trees and the heady scents of summer. On and on we hurtled through a flit of shadows towards a small sunlit aperture heralding the entrance to Jan's own little patch of Abercuawg, that medieval Welsh utopia where the cuckoos forever sing. I was extolling her evocations of Wales and the wider world, with all its concomitant melancholy, when sputtering from the radio came the news headlines: 'Gordon Brown is to hold talks with President Bush over Darfur…. More than 500 people have perished in floods and landslides in China… and Ingmar Bergman has died at his home on the Baltic.'

'Ha! Gotland!' Jan exclaimed. 'Don't I know it!'

'You've been there, then?'

'Yes, and I've been to him, too!'

I couldn't quite place them together, until Jan explained how in 1977 she'd been sent by the *New York Times* to interview Bergman, then in self-imposed exile in Munich and at work on *The Serpent's Egg*, a film about the stirrings of Nazism set in 1920s Berlin.

Trefan Morys, external view, 2007.

'It seemed to me a very hackneyed subject,' she said, swerving to avoid a fallen branch, 'and I was fool enough to say so.' She gave an airy sideways laugh. 'Bergman never forgave me… he wrote to the *New York Times*… uh, it was awful… so I sold my piece to someone else.' The director had thought Jan's questions inept and irrelevant, and she had found his answers humourless and harsh, and was unwilling to give in to the attendant sycophancy. 'I didn't like him, but then that's not the point. He was a genius without question, and at that time I hadn't seen *any* of his films.'

'Really? Rather brave of you,' I said, though in fact I thought it rather imprudent.

'Yes… was brave wasn't it,' she merrily agreed. 'No… cocky is the word.'

Her jaw juddered defiantly as we hit pothole after pothole. I began to see now in her mien some of what I'd read and heard: her pluck, her mischief, her caprice. She wasn't one to be second-guessed, and was as canny as they come. Any cockiness or smugness could be unbuttoned with chastened introspection; a disqualifying remark, a roll of the eye, a throwback of the head. Hers was a companionable laugh, a *Haha-ha!* intoned like a puzzler solving a clue, but she varied it with a disarmingly coquettish giggle that belied her age and lulled you into a false sense of intimacy. I had once seen her work an audience in this way, as she carried her eager listeners off in a single reading across waves of commas and exclamations, emphatic adjectives and chatty footnotes, down labyrinthine sentences to a faraway city, where she left us all lingering in something of a swoon. And I have seen her work an interviewer, too. One needs a plethora of questions, for her answers are quick, and quickly uttered, sometimes witty, sometimes waspish, and often qualified with a habitually mumbled and petering 'to tell you the tru...' or 'as a matter of fa...'. But truth and fact are abstruse ends for those who seek to understand the metamorphosis of James Morris – Oxonian, Soldier, Foreign Correspondent, Englishman of Empire – into Jan Trefan (her self-styled bardic name): Mystic, Essayist, Republican, Woman of Wales. 'The truth that one honours can only be one's own truth,' she said long ago, and hers has been a quest for unity, for reconciliation. Allegiances to country and sex may change, but the writer remains the same.

It was in Clevedon, Somerset, forty years before his 'at-one-ment' in a Moroccan clinic in 1972, that James Morris, cocooned beneath his mother's piano with Sibelius resounding in his ears, first realised he had been born into the wrong body. But alongside private confusion came vocational clarity and, alone on a small hill above the family home, the first inkling that he might be 'of the wandering kind'. There was much grace and promise in the myriad ships running the Bristol Channel and, with a telescope and notebook to hand, he made illustrated records of all he surveyed. The world was beckoning, so too the urge to write, and from these first fancies and conjectures came the beginnings of a book to be called *Travels with a Telescope*. I have stood on that same headland and pictured him there eagerly opening the slides of his telescope to train his gaze not only on the maritime traffic, but also the distant blue peaks which caught his eye with a 'nagging magnetism'. For across the water lay Wales, his father's country, which seemed to him then, through that misty lens, like Elysium itself.

'Now, what were you saying before,' said Jan, above the clink of loose chippings striking the chassis, 'about melancholy?'

'Well, only that I notice it, almost expect it, in your writing. Why is it *so* important to you?'

She narrowed her gaze into the middle distance. 'Don't know *why*,' she said, 'I just sort of enjoy it. I suppose hiraeth is partly it, that abstraction of unsatisfied longing for something....'

'And you wallow in it?'

'I do a bit, yeah.... I brood on it.'

As a chorister at Christ Church, Oxford in the late 1930s, James Morris' procession to the choir stalls had taken him each day beneath the glaring white-eyed bust of Robert Burton, the seventeenth-century cleric and author (under the pseudonym of Democritus Junior) of *The Anatomy of Melancholy*. Drafting his vast treatise served as a twenty-year catharsis for Burton, and one of his many and varied remedies for alleviating the black bile was a change of air. 'It will laxare animos, refresh the soul of man,' he advised, 'to see fair-built cities, streets, theatres, temples, obelisks, &c.' And yet, as becomes a contrarian, it is in such places that Jan Morris has sought not to escape 'Mistress Melancholy', but to catch her essence, and nowhere more so than in that limboid northern reach of the Adriatic. In her most celebrated work, *Venice* (1960), she devotes a whole chapter to melancholy, and the book begins and ends with it, or rather the suggestion of it, hanging over an albino lagoon. Across centuries ride Jan and Democritus in passing gondolas, he with a salutary look towards the 'goodly palaces', she plunging into the unruffled sadness of La Serenissima's neglect, into its rot and age.

The library at Trefan Morys, 2007.

Forty years on from *Venice*, and a similar wistfulness haunts the pages of *Trieste and the Meaning of Nowhere* (2001), but it is melancholy of a different strain, one of bittersweet pining, as of a homesick Welshwoman.

'Trieste isn't *in itself* melancholic,' said Jan after a time, 'just the allusions it has and the memories it holds for me make it delightfully so. It's rather naïve and childish romanticism I know, but I'm certainly not alone in thinking it of Trieste... or Wales either. Heaven knows, hiraeth has been a national characteristic forever!' Such yearnings for places, so old and full of suggestion, would seem to have always been Jan's guiding impulse. And I rather think, that every time she returned from the wider world down this old rutted track, the same frisson came with a quiver. And I felt it too, as we anticipated a final bend, and Trefan Morys, set into the lane with all the heft of an impregnable curtain wall, came narrowly into view.

'That's Twm's car,' she said pointing at a teal-coloured Morris Minor as we swung into the yard. 'Ah, and there's Elizabeth!' A short hunched-up woman in a puce smock and a wide-brimmed straw hat was just emerging from the greenery. 'Well, here *he* is,' said Jan, slamming the car door and motioning at me, 'and here *we* are.' She took a faltering step back and made a great showy sweep of her arm. '*This* is our house!' Elizabeth's deep eyes crinkled.

'One comes, and one goes,' she said, nodding quaintly.

So palpable is Trefan Morys in Jan's writings that it felt like a return for me, too. For good measure, I patted the stone and followed them in through the blue stable door. Elizabeth removed her hat, ran a hand through her grey bob, and clutched Jan gently by the wrist.

'Look at this,' she whispered, taking from her pocket a sheeny black feather and twizzling it triumphantly between her fingers. 'Two ravens, just gone in.'

'Oh good! So they *are* nesting!'

I watched this happy little exchange from the corner, beneath a large print of a liner entering Manhattan. Ravens pair for life, do they not? The ladies began to rustle up tea in something of a dansant, amidst a whirl of jangling pans, marmalade pots, wine bottles and cat bowls. I was staring at the plasterwork with its scribbled telephone numbers and grandchildren's measurements when Jan beckoned me over.

'Now, you were wanting a tour of the library, yes?' she said, pushing open a scrubbed pine door onto a view that put one in mind of a Vermeer or de Hooch. 'Come look at them….'

Save for the curl of an olive-green chair, a low-slung monochrome room stretched away some forty feet hence. Columns of shelving sprung up from a great chessboard floor, onto which I followed Jan, like a pawn trailing the Queen. She pointed out markers in her life: near to hand was her grandfather's copy of *The Adventures of Huckleberry*

Finn (the first book she could remember reading) and up there – I followed the line of her arm – was *Alexandria: A History and a Guide* by EM Forster, whose maxim 'to wander aimlessly' had long been Jan's, too. Murray and Baedeker guides, strewn over maps on a plan chest, hinted at imminent departures, and close by was a separate shelf for books with introductions by Jan.

'I did hundreds once, didn't I, Elizabeth?' she called out without waiting for a response, 'mostly to old imperialists doing their memoirs, you know.' Our chess moves continued. 'These are biographies – I'm very keen on letters and diaries – this is *all* Venice, and this *entire* wall,' she said, throwing up her arms as if readying an orchestra, 'is the British Empire.'

Inspecting these ranks of books in close order, their raised bands like epaulettes, you could almost smell the khaki drill, or expect to hear a distant bugle call or the shrilling of a peacock on the veranda. I was drawn to a well-thumbed line-up on my right which I knew at once to be a favoured shelf. Here, shoulder-to-shoulder stood TE Lawrence, Alexander Kinglake and Charles Doughty, those travelling scholars of a bygone age who had called to the adolescent James Morris from the deserts of Arabia. And it wasn't long before he had followed in their sandy footsteps, firstly in 1943 as an intelligence officer in the 9th Queen's Royal Lancers, later as a journalist, and with something of the same haughty outlook. 'It was difficult for any Englishman,' Morris wrote in 1957, 'however liberal his sympathies, to resist the illusion that he was somebody special in the Middle East, somebody to whom the normal rules did not apply, a being apart and divinely favoured. I knew this sensation well… a deep-rooted imperial instinct.'

I pointed at the faded nut-orange spine of *Eothen* (1844) by Kinglake, a book whose pervading gentlemanly humour and frank impressions of its author's travels in the Turkish Near East had captivated Jan since schooldays, and led her to acknowledge him as 'my master'.

'May I?'

She handed it to me gingerly, saying it had been a gift from Elizabeth, and I opened it carefully to see evidence of this on the flyleaf: 'To James Morris, With so much love on this our ninth wedding anniversary, from Elizabeth, 18th March 1958.' I knew the books on this shelf to be milestones in the pantheon of English 'travel writing', a label Jan had resisted all her life, but she was drawn to them not for their genre, more their style. 'It is not the travel that is important in *Eothen*,' she once wrote, 'only the traces it left upon its author's very particular sensibility.' She could have been describing herself. Kinglake had adopted an epistolary form – *Eothen* is addressed to 'one of his friends' – and I reminded Jan of Patrick Leigh Fermor once telling me that he too wrote with someone in mind, a considered friend who should read it, and like it. Did she ever write for others?

'No. I write *entirely* for myself,' she said without hesitation. 'It's *all* autobiography, the whole thing. I've written forty books. It's entirely selfish and egocentric.' It was the kind of halting frankness to quell further questions, and she seemed to relish my bewildered expression. But if her books were just one long self-indulgence, then wasn't it doubly fortunate that readers had invested such interest?

'Yes, amazing!' she exclaimed with wide-eyed incredulity, as if no-one had ever noticed. Not only did Jan write solely for her own pleasure but she also extolled the virtues of travelling alone.

'You said once that your moments of supreme happiness and sudden ecstasy have been solitary ones?'

'Y-e-s,' she agreed tentatively, 'but I don't think that's true of Paddy, as a matter of fa…. He's much more sociable than I am. He loves meeting people. I don't, particularly.'

A curious admission from a collector of cities, unless one keeps in mind the self-regarding example of Kinglake: the outsider, the onlooker, heeding only to one's own instincts. But isn't a place its people, I thought. 'Surely to get a flavour of a city, you need to interact?'

'You do... a bit... yes,' she replied with a swither, before reeling off her various traveller's methods for striking up conversations with strangers, such as the smile test, or asking for directions she already knew. 'So yes, in that way of course I do, but I think Paddy loves people, he loves exploring them, finding out how they work. I don't care. I'm only interested in the impression they make upon me, and that's why he's a better writer. I admit it!'

She was not only shutting out scrutiny, but appeared to be resolving a comparison I had never made, though perhaps many others had? Only yesterday, she'd had a letter from an admirer who said her writing reminded them of Leigh Fermor's, but she wasn't having any of it, and nor was I. Whatever else, she was a frenetic wordsmith, schooled in the urgency of reportage and deadlines, Leigh Fermor a scholarly perfectionist, unhurried by time. In the course of a day, Jan might manage twelve pages, Paddy might alter a comma. Was speed of the essence?

'His is a more profound mind than mine,' she said in summation. 'Much cleverer, better informed... the only thing we have in common is a sense of joie de vivre.'

I handed back her cherished copy of *Eothen* and as she slid it back into its place, I asked her what sort of influence these writers had made on her.

'I don't believe in influences,' came her brusque reply. I tried a different tack, mentioning how Leigh Fermor had picked out *Old Calabria* (1915) by Norman Douglas as the quintessential travel book for him. Jan pattered her pointed nails across the row of book spines and picked out a scuffed grey volume with blue embossing.

'Well, this,' she acceded, 'is the quintessential book for me!'

It was one of several editions she owned of *Travels in Arabia Deserta* (1888) by Charles Doughty. 'I *love* this book,' she said clasping it sacredly to her chest. 'I bought it long, long ago in Steimatzky's in Jerusalem at the end of the war.' And 'old Doughty', as she referred to it, had been her pick-me-up ever since; a near devotional book from which to pick passages at random and recite them as an arcane incantation, and none more so than its opening paragraph which long ago she had set to a melody of her own composing. She said she was apt to singing it, often in the bath, and without opening the book, she began to cantillate the words, 'A new voice hailed me of an old friend when, first returned from the Peninsula, I paced again in that long street of Damascus which is called Straight….' She went on in a voice of quivering elocuted lightness that seemed to seep through her teeth, and reaching the last line, 'What moved thee, or how couldst thou take such journeys into the fanatic Arabia?' she rounded it off with a triumphant syllable. And in that hailing of *'Arabi-ah!'* I saw how Doughty's prose, alongside Lawrence's and Kinglake's, never failed to halt the sands of time and transport her back to a desert wilderness of youth.

She held 'old Doughty' up to her nose and inhaled deeply.

'American edition. Can you smell it?' she asked handing it to me, 'the ink….'

But I could sense only a must of mildew.

'You'll have to take my word for it,' she smiled, placing it back and pointing to a further recess. 'Now that *entire* corner contains American books and sometimes when I stand there I can actually smell that obsolete printer's ink without taking a book out. Maybe it's all in my mind but it reminds me of Corsican wine, because every now and then if you buy a crate, one or two bottles will have that heavenly scent of the mountains.'

It was one of those sensory pleasures so redolent of her prose, and yet even without the aroma of Mediterranean vineyards, I was already in the throes of bibliomania. Had I more time and freer reign, I would have browsed these shelves exhaustively, but this private library of more than eight thousand books, many of them with tempting protrusions of cuttings and letters, would be the privilege of a future archivist. Did Elizabeth mind her home being given over to books?

'Well, it's a bit of a bore for her, because it's only a small house,' Jan's eyebrows sloped in sympathy then danced in jest, 'but I suppose she's got to lump it.' She mouthed a silent laugh, and then straightened a section on battleships. Did she ever have a culling?

'Oh, I should, I should,' she said with mock weariness. But I felt she had long ceased to be her library's keeper, that the house itself had since become a self-accreting entity, intent on amassing further books to caulk its foundations and bind its walls, and satisfy its custodian in her dotage. 'There's a publisher that sends me every book they ever print,' she pointed to a pile on a far table, 'and most of them, for my money, are unreadable.' Yet there they remained, along with surplus paperbacks of her own back catalogue. 'Have you got that?' she asked, picking up a new edition of her only novel, *Hav*. I hadn't. 'Try it,' she thrust it into my hand, 'might amuse you, to skim through.'

Shuffling a little, she led me on across the great expanse of linoleum where there had once been cobblestones. I said I'd always taken pleasure in the placing of books, their arrangement upon a shelf, and the synergy of disparate authors meeting side by side.

'They give off something, don't you think?'

'Well, this is your fantasy, not mine,' she replied, peering over her glasses, though she had, she admitted, taken the 'impertinent' pleasure of placing a signed copy of John Ruskin's *Stones of Venice* beside a copy of her own book about the city. She said she was a sucker for signed volumes, but held first editions in no regard and at one time – I was horrified to learn – used to discard their dust jackets.

'I've just done something which I'm slightly ashamed of,' she muttered. 'Long ago, in the London Library, I happened to run into Bruce Chatwin when I had with me his first book, *In Patagonia*. He signed it 'For Jan Morris, in the London Library', and then the other day I got overwhelmed with money and demands to build a sort of little writing dacha around the corner here for Twm, so I sold the book... I wasn't awfully keen on it, to tell you the tru... but I must say, it got me a lot of money.'

There was however one book here which was beyond price, and beyond parting with, and related to the other defining moment in Jan's life, when as *The Times* correspondent James Morris on the 1953 Mount Everest expedition, he had managed to relay, by coded telegram, the news of its conquest just in time for Coronation Day. She pulled from a shelf not her own book about the expedition, but a ragged yellow proof copy of *The Story of Everest* by WH Murray. It had been sent for review just before departing for the Himalayas, and so had been taken to be signed by every member of the team as a memento. She lifted out a wad of brittle tanned cuttings folded inside the cover to reveal a column of heroic names, from John Hunt's long flourish at the top to Edmund Hillary's large scrawl lower down.

'Wylie died a week ago,' she said, tapping her finger on his name, 'just five of us left now, I think.' She thumbed through the book, and edged from its pages a small signed photograph of a man with fulgent eyes and a broad moustachioed smile whom I knew at once to be the Sherpa guide, Tenzing Norgay.

'And those are Tibetan terriers,' she said, referring to the dogs under his arms, 'given to him by the Dalai Lama, so he told me.' Jan had joined up with Tenzing, as they descended from 23,000 feet. 'We sat and had breakfast together beneath the Khumbu glacier, and as a souvenir he took this out from his wallet.' The photograph trembled in her hand, and she seemed for a moment to be stepping with a pang back onto those frozen screes. 'I asked him to sign it for me, and 'Tenzing' was the *only* word he could write…. Ah, he was a princely figure, one of nature's aristocrats, and I thought *this* was the most noble signature. He was in very high spirits – he'd just climbed Everest after all! – and he was on his way to a neighbouring village to tell his old mother the news.'

Everest changed Morris from an unknown twenty-six-year-old journalist into the most famous reporter in the world, and looking down at her keepsakes, I complimented her on such an auspicious start to her career.

'Yes, it was rather good wasn't it,' she said putting a hand to her heart and bowing her head. 'Well, there we are....' and she slapped the book shut and returned it to a section on mountains.

Beyond Everest, James Morris traversed America and soon left *The Times* for the *Manchester Guardian,* where he secured his next big scoop, revealing a collusion between British, French and Israeli forces during the Suez Crisis. But in 1962 he began a retreat from what he saw as the man-made turmoil of the world, from its coups and revolutions, and its great wars which had ravaged and killed close relatives. He resigned his position as a foreign correspondent, relabelled himself a belle-lettrist and set sail across the sex divide. A South African witch doctor had told him that he was going to change, going to obey the voices in his head, going to be 'different'. And so it proved. Between 1964 and 1972, he swallowed some 12,000 pills and absorbed 50,000 milligrams of 'female matter' in a bid to escape manhood. The male form had become repugnant to him, as had a man's passions and instincts. Even the memory of Everest became tainted, for whilst he retained a patriotic pride in its conquest, he found it hard to separate from the sham virility and muscular ambition of it all. But however conflicted, however ambivalent he might have felt, he couldn't quite give up on the lure and trappings of empire, on its once swanky grandeur and slow melancholic decay, and he retained a wry and reverential sympathy for it that no amount of pills or hormone enhancement could assuage. Perhaps its conceit and swagger were nostalgically and irredeemably ingrained? Was there not an imperious stance in seizing a place, be it mountain or city, encapsulating it and making it yours forever? Gradually though, he started to believe not in the strength of large nations but in the serenity of small ones. Wales would be his antidote to imperialism, and whilst he began to recognise and honour the Cymreictod, the Welshness that was part of his patrimony, it was at first with the detachment of the Anglo–Welsh. A letter from Plaid Cymru's general secretary JE Jones forced a change of attitude. Jones had found Morris' early articles on Wales equivocal, and he urged him (in something of a recruiting drive by the party) to cease being an outsider and write as an active participant. It was a clarion call, and Morris vacillated no more, writing with new-found fervour under such headings as *Why I Am a Welsh Nationalist*.

The clank of a ship's bell signalled the fleeting visit of the postman.

'You've got three identical envelopes from *Granta*,' called Elizabeth, 'and two books.'

'Ha! I must check,' said Jan, making for the kitchen. 'I'm expecting one from Gregynog....'

Elizabeth handed me two large cushions and, taking the tea tray, she led me up a narrow spiral staircase, and – by way of a low window – out onto a small slated terrace. I slouched down and told her I was glad to have finally made it here.

'Well, I hope you aren't disappointed,' she said. 'They come and they write these things, and take pictures, and it's always a bit false....' She adjusted her hat, to ward off the sun from a recent procedure on her cheek. 'It's a lovely place, because we're miles from anyone, except the Parrys over at the farm, and they're awfully nice, so if anybody comes down the lane they're usually walkers who've lost their way.'

I asked her about their former home, Plas Trefan, which I kept glimpsing through the veil of oaks above the yard.

'Clough found it,' she said, lifting up a tea cosy in the form of a thatched cottage.

During that period in the early 1960s, their spidery old friend, Clough Williams-Ellis, had managed to gather around his Italianate folly Portmeirion – largely as tenants – a coterie of writers and radicals. The Morrises were then living in Oxford but renting a cottage near him at Llanfrothen.

'He said there was a house down here which he thought would suit us. It hadn't been lived in for some time and this stable-block was more or less a ruin.... But we found that once the children had grown up,

The Plas was far too big. So we sold it and the land over there, but kept an island in the river and this building. And that,' she added, pointing across the lane, 'that used to be our garage and we turned it into a house for Twm.'

The move from The Plas, the manor house to the bwthyn, this worker's dwelling, seemed symbolic of new loyalties, and I reminded myself that, aside from wanting to see Jan's library, I was keen to discuss her Welsh origins and espousals. I could hear cheery whistling from inside the house. Sheep doddered in the meadow, a man with a small white dog passed by and a gentle southerly breeze assailed us with a reek of silage.

'Well, here we are, five minutes before the rain.' Jan emerged in a blaze of sunny yellow splendour, brandishing a paper knife. 'Et voila!' she exclaimed, slicing open the end of her parcel and just missing me in the process.

'Ha! I nearly stabbed you!' she said with a quick throaty laugh.

'That would have been a short interview....'

'Short life for me too, they'd put me in jail. Even shorter for you,' she pointed the blade at me, 'you'd be a corpse, haha-ha!'

Done with murdering her house guest, she turned her attention to the book in hand, a new edition of Wilfred Owen's poems and letters entitled *Mapping Golgotha*, which bore all the hallmarks of Gregynog Press' exacting standards. The hand-sewn cloth boards, bound in quarter calfskin with silk end-bands, were of a sulphurous hue and depicted lines of soldiers silhouetted ominously in no-man's land. It seemed an opportune moment. Jan had once written fleetingly of her own father being 'gassed for his empire' during the Great War, and I longed to know more about him, since it was his Welsh blood that coursed through Jan and had surely made Wales the country of her heart.

'I don't much like the colour,' she said.

'Mustard gas,' I responded.

She peered at me over the top of the book, reclined her head a little and narrowed her eyes. 'Yes, quite true, it's full of allusions....'

Elizabeth poured out tea, and I thought about the little I knew of Jan's antecedents. From afar, her parents seemed a curious, sudden match of Norman and Celtic stock. Devout and cosmopolitan, Enid Payne was possessed of a gift for music (she had trained as a concert pianist at the Leipzig Conservatoire) that in different aspects passed to her three children. Walter Morris, eleven years her junior, had been raised in a pub in Monmouth, as one of fourteen children, and was an engineer with fair prospects, until the Great War poisoned and broke him, body and mind. Thereafter, married to Enid and living in Clevedon, he became a distant and nebulous figure, sometimes employed as a taxi driver, though largely confined to a convalescent home. But what of *his* Wales, I kept asking myself, what of the stories and songs of his homeland? What, if any of it, had he imparted to his youngest child? Given that he died soon after Jan turned twelve, perhaps very little, and yet fragments can be found in her writings. She recalls somewhere the cadence of his voice, a Welsh-inflected English, and his affection for the sentimental ballad. Elsewhere, she tells of his birthplace, within sight of Pen-y-fâl, on whose flanks his 'decent proud people' had always lived, some of them still speaking the old language. And sometimes, when on her travels, she suddenly finds 'an integrity and earnestness of thought' remindful of the life her forebears led 'on the intellectual fringes of country society near the Welsh border'. This was a birthright she would embrace as certainly as her new sex, so why had her father remained a footnote? Had no-one ever enquired? Was it simply enough that he *was* Welsh, and that in claiming Wales, she had reclaimed him too? I looked at Jan, who was still skimming through the Gregynog book, and told her I had a few specific questions. She heaved a sigh.

'I hope they're not things about,' she stopped and rephrased, 'well, what *are* they about?'

'Welshness,' I began, 'comes through your father's side....'

She hummed in agreement.

'And yet you make very little mention of him.' She hummed again, but in a brisker tone. 'You've said somewhere that he sprang from the ranks of the gwerin – meaning?'

'Meaning the mass of the Welsh people, the simple folk, though others see it as the peasantry. It's a very outdated term but it used to be common among nationalists of an earlier generation.'

'And without that heritage,' I said, gesturing to Wales at large, 'you wouldn't have all of this....'

'No, sure,' she nodded.

'So I'm intrigued to know more about him; about *his* Wales, *his* Welshness.'

There was a telling pause, and a drifting of eyes. 'No,' she said abruptly with a twitch of her mouth. 'No, I don't want to talk about that, anyway.' Elizabeth let out an uncertain giggle.

'May I ask why?'

Jan's forefinger began to patrol her lower lip with the regularity of a metronome. 'No,' she repeated, dismissively now, 'I don't talk about my mother, either. I don't want to talk about *any* of them.' Leaning forward, her beads swinging pendulously between us, she prodded her chest, and told me straight, 'Life begins with *me*!'

I didn't quite follow this four-word slogan, declaimed in clipped and deepening tones, but I felt the exclamation mark. Whatever did it mean? Was this a declaration of the self-invented, or re-invented, or self-possessed?

'Kraa-kraa' came rasping laughter from the trees, and – looking away from Jan – I caught not Elizabeth's shaded eyes but the serene gaze from a bronze bust on the parapet which, with all its youthful angularity, seemed to me to be of Jan's former self. It was, for a moment that bristled with unease, like Janus incarnate, that old transitional deity who looked to the past with one face and to the future with another. But whilst one smiled benignly, the other was clenched with mistrust. Perhaps Jan sensed a coming impertinence or some pseudo-Freudian inquiry or had become unnerved by my folder of notes. Elizabeth stifled another laugh and began to collect our cups. One comes, and one goes, I rather suppose she was thinking to herself as she departed with the tea-tray.

'It's a love affair with Wales really, isn't it?' I said, thinking still of Jan's father as a spur for her love of country, but she seemed even less inclined to agree with anything I suggested now.

'Sort of… well… no,' she trailed off, 'it's a love affair with *her*!' She gestured after Elizabeth. 'We've lived together for fifty-five years or something… it all goes together for me. That's why I don't want to talk about things further back. It *all* begins with *me*.'

In her book *The Matter of Wales* (1984), Jan devotes no less than three pages to the many Morrises throughout its history. Her namesake, she maintained, had always been ubiquitous in the affairs of Wales. I reminded her of this list, and she began to spell out its variants. 'M-O-R-U-S, M-O-R-Y-S, M-O-R-I-S, M-O-R-R-I-S…' she chimed, adding how her children had adopted different iterations.

'And do they all flock back here still?'

She shook her head. 'We email all the time,' she said, referring to her two elder sons, 'but they don't come…. One's Canadian now, teaches at the University of Alberta, written a very learned book about contemporary classical music…. Then I've got one in Spain. He's an occultist, travels a lot, devoted to this Maharaji….' A daughter went unmentioned, but Jan's youngest son Twm seemed to be something of a mesmeric alter ego. He and Jan had collaborated on books and translations, and his poetic sorcery, his weaving of cynghanedd, had caused her to liken him to a wizard. He in turn had likened her to a unicorn. Theirs was a mystical bond, the enchanter and the enchanted. In a similar chimeric vein, Jan was fond of ascribing her bodily transition to magic. Welsh mythology is replete with stories of regeneration and transformation, from the poet and shaman Taliesin assuming multiple forms, to the Tylwyth Teg replacing mortals with crimbilion or changelings. Had Jan not exchanged one soul for another? Or combined both? Had she not practised her own lore, and through pills and surgery rather than herbs and spells, attained the gift of shapeshifting? She was a changeling, was she not, who appeared to be living happily ever after.

Here at Trefan Morys she had embedded herself in a Welsh-speaking hinterland far from the anglicised border country of her father, and I made this point openly in the hope it might elicit something more. It didn't, though she was clearly fed up with the historical antipathy that still lingered between the country's extremities.

'If only we could make it more of a unity,' she said trenchantly, 'that's the thing I do feel. I'm passionately keen to close the gap between north and south, for example I won't use a capital "N" for north, in fact I won't use "North", I always say "northern Wales".'

But a new sense of unity was already in the air, given the momentous political manoeuvres of the past few weeks, from which a new 'One Wales' coalition had been formed between Labour and Plaid Cymru. Mention of it brought a rush of elation.

'Oh my gosh! Well of course I was so excited when the rainbow coalition came in May. I thought this is a *new* beginning, a *real* beginning, and maybe it still will be…?' It had given her cause to dream again of Abercuawg, and of the cuckoos stirring in that ancient and unsullied Welsh idyll. Might its time be nearing? Might we be on the cusp of it? 'We're short of cuckoos here,' she said dreamily, 'but you can still hear them in Cwm Pennant.' She looked to the fields. 'I mean it's halfway there, isn't it?' she said in the hope that a reconciliation might be achieved between the two parties and their separate ambitions. She told me that she had just submitted a piece to *The Guardian* reflecting on this new dawn of possibility, but with some reservation. It had been ten years since devolution and yet for her the Welsh Assembly was still mired in drab and unimaginative officialdom, lacking in charisma or the 'fire and fun of a march towards fulfilment'. For her and others in this far north-west, a Labour-headed Assembly ruling from Cardiff still seemed 'not just physically, but temperamentally remote'.

She longed for history to repeat itself, for an independent Wales embodied within a federal Europe, governed centrally from a new national capital in Machynlleth, just as the rebel leader Owain Glyndŵr had done at the turn of the fifteenth century when he had summoned his Senedd there and proclaimed himself Tywysog Cymru. It is in his spirit, in his *company,* she would have it, that Jan made her fervent encomiums for a once and future Wales. She had left the 'hard tack' campaigning, as she put it, to the politicians, and yet, like Dafydd Iwan (who once took refuge here at The Plas after his release from prison in 1970), she remained a 'poetic agitator' who could still ruffle feathers. Less than a week after my visit, one Welsh Labour MP, responding to Jan's opinion piece in *The Guardian*, took issue with her 'cultural nationalist clique' and its suggestions of a 'quasi-fascistic rural idyll'. For him and others, hers was ornate and mawkish sentiment, too proud and nostalgic, too much hwyl and hiraeth. But not for me. I knew Jan's Wales to be a country in the mind, a timeless and illusory one, that had healed her inner wounds and enabled her to find herself. And I felt a bracing affinity in conjuring a Wales of one's very own, for me a land poignant with memories and potent with melancholy in all its dreamy lyricism and mystical otherness.

'If you love something hotly enough, consciously, with care,' she wrote of Wales in 1974, 'it becomes yours by symbiosis, irrevocably.' Two years later, patriot had turned extremist, and she was proudly nailing her colours to the mast. 'I have progressed in stages to the conviction that Wales must be as independent as the Republic of Ireland,' she declared in a letter to her old employer *The Times,* 'and I positively look forward to the day when the United Kingdom no longer exists.' Was she, I wondered, still so vehement? Without glancing at my notes I threw out another old quote in which she had described herself as a 'republican nationalist'. She bristled. 'I… I don't think I've ever called myself a 'republican nationalist' as a matter of fa.... I've called myself all sorts of republican things, but there's a disagreeable aspect to nationalism, isn't there? It's aggressive, and boastful, and intrusive, and is really rather unpleasant.' She was relishing her adjectives again. 'Whereas patriotism seems to me something rather noble, something honourable and generous and not aggressive at all. So that's why I don't like the word.'

I made time to find the quote and corrected myself. It was 'Welsh Nationalist Republican' and it had appeared in an article by her in the *Evening Standard,* 1 July, 1997, to mark the handover of Hong Kong, and with it perhaps an end to her own preoccupation with empire.

'Ah well, it's because "nationalist" was of course a political term then, wasn't it, a specific one about the Welsh Nationalist Party, and I was a nationalist in that sense, *of course.* But it's true as I get older I've grown to detest the nation state.' Her forefinger began to patrol her lower lip again. 'But that's a different thing.... It's an unfair quote of yours, because in that context I was thinking about Plaid Cymru.'

There was the thudding of a door somewhere off, and a tractor starting up. The stone was giving out a dull hard heat, and we both seemed struck with inertia. Jan noticed me staring at another bronze bust on the parapet.

'Come,' she said pointing at it. 'I'll show you something apropos of *him*, Admiral Jacky Fisher, with whom I am going to have an affair in the afterlife!'

The dingy coolness of her bedroom revived us. Against one wall, yet more books in stacks of varying heights formed a teetering paperback metropolis, and on the coverlet, splayed open like small tents, were *The Radetsky March* by Joseph Roth and *The General in His Labyrinth* by Gabriel Garcia Marquez.

'I've always got something on the go,' she said, 'but the more I read, the more I feel I can't waste my time on contemporary books when there are great works waiting to be re-read, and I forget books very quickly. It's

Jan with Jacky Fisher, 2007.

an awful thing to say, but most contemporary writing I can't be bothered with…. Now then,' she said, demanding my attention. 'Whenever I have visitors to this house, I do this to them,' and with a stagey glissade and a 'dum-de-de-dum', she swung open her wardrobe door to reveal a large photograph of the self-same bug-eyed Admiral. He looked poutingly indignant at his dark and solitary confinement, and I was at a loss for words, but then what does one say when an octogenarian trans woman shows you their pin-up?

'D'you know,' she said, filling the awkward silence, 'Beryl Bainbridge had this experience foisted on her, and all she said was, "What tiny ears he's got". Well, really….' And with that Jan bade the admiral goodnight and returned him to the comfort of her dresses.

A low gnarly doorway gave onto a living room which matched the downstairs library only in length. Bamboo loungers and haggard sofas with pinkish zig-zagged upholstery were clustered around a central woodstove and, above us, Porthmadog schooners sailed silently along oaken shipping lanes that criss-crossed the eaves. In the near corner was a pedestal desk with green leather inlay, and behind it a sturdy bardic chair with handbags slung across its fretwork. This is where she wrote at will, where the words were summoned, and where more than thirty of her books had been drafted, and re-drafted, and declaimed to the room, or even sung into shape in the manner of 'old Doughty'. I imagined, that in some transmuted way, all those spoken words were still captive here, vibrating in the air, or resonant in the walls, so that some aspect of all those far-off places lingered here too. Here was all the world in a Welsh hayloft.

It was only now that I noticed Jan's own books, which seemed to issue straight from her writing desk in a great long assembly line along the outer wall of the room. They formed a spectrum of transformation: James to the left, Jan to the right, and in the middle a confusion of Morrises.

'Well, here they all are,' she said, adjusting her glasses. 'And that's pure, pure egocentricity! I keep every single edition, you know. Most are there beyond merit… but I *gloat* over them!'

'And do you dip back into them?'

'Occasionally, yes, I do.'

'For reference? Pleasure?'

'Just for pleasure, really, I chiefly dip back into *Trieste* because I'm proudest of that. It was consciously and deliberately my last book, and I set out everything that I wanted to be put in there about me… rather like talking to you, ha-hah…. I certainly didn't tell all, but I was freer talking about myself in that book than I have been in any of the others.' Freer, but no less concealed, I thought, and still hovering diffidently between candour and caginess. She had once declared evasions to be aesthetic rather than secretive, in itself the most slithery of explanations. I had become lost in her multitudes, and tantalised by her sidesteps. I told her she seemed to me aloof, hard to pin down.

'Well, yes… I don't want to….' she clicked hesitantly. 'There are parts of myself… I want to *keep* private.'

'And that's a conscious act?'

'No, not particularly,' came her wan and slightly huffy deflection. And did she still think of herself as an outsider?

'Oh yes, I like to be an outsider. Not quite so much as I used to, though….'

'And why's that?'

'Oh I don't know…. I suppose I got used to being me.'

She gave her coquettish giggle and wandered off towards a far window that looked out onto the vegetable garden. I stared back at her books, and from them plucked out a rarity, one that had eluded all my searches, a children's book no less, the *only* children's book by Jan.

'What do you have there?'

'*The Upstairs Donkey*,' I said, holding it up.

'Ah yes, now as a matter of fa… I first came across that story when I was Middle East correspondent on *The Times*. A man, can't remember his name, British Arabophile, friend of the king of Jordan, it was he ƒ who told me the story of the Upstairs Donkey. Then I adapted some more folk tales, and made that little book out of them…. It was nicely done, illustrated by Pauline Baynes, who was at that time a rather distinguished illustrator…. Might be worth printing again, you never know, except there's something in it I thought was rather unsuitable for children, something a bit *too* bloodthirsty: disembowelment and such like.'

She sat in the nook and began to pick cobwebs off a piece of Armenian pottery. I walked over and held up my camera.

'Make sure you get that in,' she said, referring to the crack in the plaster. 'Clough used to have them put in artificially, you know….'

She glanced through the window and hummed contentedly as she caught sight of Elizabeth with a weeding trug below. Her lips began to form into a whistle, but she caught herself, called a halt and was about to get up when I insisted on taking a couple of further, closer portraits.

'Funny,' she balked, 'you're the first person that's *ever* done that to me. I usually say, well, that's it now, and they *always* limply agree.' And the way she said 'limply' in rather disappointed tones made me wish I'd pressed harder with some of my queries. 'Here, how about an un-melancholic one,' and she beamed into the lens.

We returned to the inky moulder of the ground floor by a set of wide wooden stairs, and we did so cautiously for it was down these very stairs that Jan had fallen the year before, landing her up in hospital and requiring brain surgery.

'It was trepanning,' she said, patting her woolly scalp as we reached the bottom, 'what the Incas did, you know. But, as a matter of fa… it didn't work, I wasn't compos mentis… so I had to have a second op.'

She was tired and her health, she said, holding onto the banister, had been rather unpredictable since then. Her recuperation had prevented her from picking up the new Worldwide Welsh Award for services to Wales abroad, and so, belatedly, she was off in a few days to the Mold Eisteddfod to receive it. The trophy, along with a Celtic torc, was no doubt destined for this devotedly Welsh section of her library where we loitered, glared at by red kites and red foxes from their opaque vitrines.

Here too, at our feet, stood a small slate plaque of a very different order, but a familiar one. For thirty years, copiously mentioned and gasconaded, a premature farewell had been subsumed into the fabric of the house. For this was Jan and Elizabeth's gravestone, a marker not so much of departure as devotion, and as totemic as a lovespoon. Their names, finely etched by the artist Jonah Jones, sat boldly above a Celtic cross within a circle of eternity, and yet it occurred to me, reading the epitaph – 'Yma Mae Dwy Ffrind ar Derfyn Un Bywyd * Here Are Two Friends at the End of One Life' – that it could just as well have referred to Jan alone. How about that, I thought, for a lasting touch of ambiguity. How typical of a completist to round off her life with a carefully composed valedictory. Or so I thought until she happened to mention, quite casually, that she would be signing off for good with a collection of allegorical musings in a 'final' book, to be published posthumously.

'Will you sign my visitors' book?' she asked, pulling one out from a heap on the central table. 'They take ten years to fill, but I don't think I'll be here that long, so I'm going backwards in the same book.' She located the last entry, just as Elizabeth called from the kitchen. 'Now, how about there, next to that drawing by Iwan Bala?' and she left me to it.

As I flicked back through decades of encounters, it struck me, from the names on show, how Trefan Morys had itself become a destination for the travel writers who had followed in Jan's wake. There was Theroux, and Thubron, and Wheeler and Winchester, amongst scores of Welsh surnames, many grangerised with thin confident line drawings by Jan herself. I could hear chatter from the kitchen: Did you see? He's brought us the back end of a mouse again…. For God's sake, we've all been to Berlin, and we don't want to hear any traveller's tales, and even as I said it I thought this was unkind…. Well, I rang him this morning to say sorry, but he didn't seem to notice…. Glass of wine? And as all these names slipped through my fingers, overlaid by Jan and Elizabeth's jovial banter and the pop of a cork and the clink of glass on ringed fingers, it suddenly put me in mind of those benevolent hostesses of an earlier age, the Ladies of Llangollen, and how like them, Jan and Elizabeth – the Ladies of Llanystumdwy if you will – ushered in all those who beat a path to their door: friends, admirers, strangers, inquisitors, the plain curious. And me.

I felt something brush my leg.

'Ah, you've met Ibsen,' said Jan returning to the room. 'We've had dozens of cats,' she hoisted him up, 'but *never* one like this. He's a Norwegian forest cat, you know. Double coat. Gets very shaggy in the winter.' She said a house without a cat is a house lacking, before coyly admitting that it was tripping over Ibsen last year that had sent her down those back stairs. They narrowed their eyes at one another in skittish complicity.

'I love him with his ears back like this,' said Jan holding him close, his paws flexing on her beads, 'dear old friend.'

We wandered out into the yard. Shafts of sunlight had pierced the house and were forming brilliant ellipses in the gravel. It was getting on for a pleasant evening, and I fancied walking off our long chat, so I gratefully declined the offer of a lift back to the village and a glass of wine and another paperback. I wished them both well, and as the Ladies of Llanystumdwy waved me off, a flash of tawny white darted into the bushes, ravens took flight, sheep bleated, and was that a cuckoo calling in the woods?

Nearing a turn in the lane, and feeling Trefan Morys to be receding from view, I looked back. And there was Jan, atop the terrace again, looking seaward. And she seemed to me in that moment a beacon, a commanding streak of monochrome stripes, like a lighthouse on a breakwater at the entrance to one of those many ports through which she had passed so often. She might very well be standing at the Punta della Dogana in Venice, or before the Narrows in Manhattan, or upon Bradleys Head facing Sydney Harbour, or perhaps beneath the Miramare in Trieste, forever waving to the boats bearing travellers forth. Or she might just be looking out from Wain's Hill on the northern shore of Somerset, having just clambered up through the woods and bracken with a notebook and telescope to hand.

She was whistling, too.

Jan with Ibsen, 2007.

Postscript

Like many, I loosely wondered what might be imparted, or revealed, in
the posthumous book she'd mentioned to me in our meeting of late July.
But, as it turned out, I did not have to wait for *Allegorizings*, because
there in a diary (*Thinking Again*, Faber) published just seven months
before her death in November 2020, came a brief mournful entry that
satisfied any lingering questions I still had regarding her patrimony: 'The

most vivid memory I have of [my father]', she wrote, 'finds him fitfully asleep in bed one afternoon when I was home from school on holiday. In his dreams the war was raging still, and when I crept awestruck into his bedroom he cried out warnings, tossed and turned, moaned and coughed uncontrollably and sometimes bitterly laughed, so alive in his nightmare that I heard the guns myself, ducked to the screaming whistle of the shells, smelt the cordite and the treacherous, murderous gas.... My father has never quite died for me, though. I hardly knew him, but when I think of him, I am with him still, at his side, on that day of war in Flanders.'

MR Thomas is an award-winning documentary filmmaker, formerly for BBC Arts and now freelance. For the past thirty years, he has been interviewing and photographing the writers and artists of Wales. A correspondence with Jan Morris over several years led to this visit in late July 2007.

DAWN CHORUS, VESPER FLIGHTS

YVONNE REDDICK ON THREE BROAD-RANGING NATURE
ESSAY COLLECTIONS BY WOMEN WHICH EXPLORE
ANTHROPOMORPHISM, GRIEF, 'MANSPLAINING' AND
THE NECESSARY LIMITS SET BY NEMESIS

HELEN MACDONALD, JASMINE DONAHAYE AND JAY GRIFFITHS FIND
moving, intriguing and surprising ways to connect with the natural
world. From lanes and meadows in Wales and Surrey, to the Atacama
Desert, the forests of West Papua and the Bay Area of California, these
striking essays weave in crucial themes: extinction; climate change;
racism; an underreported genocide; lying politicians; male domination,
domestic abuse. Crafting an essay collection is a delicate art, and these
authors succeed in creating essays that work as standalone pieces and
which answer one another as part of a whole.

'These are terrible times for the environment,' writes Helen
Macdonald in her much-anticipated essay collection, *Vesper Flights*. If
Macdonald's celebrated book *H is for Hawk* explored the process of grieving for her father while training her falconry goshawk Mabel, the grief
and wonder in this book spring from our relationship with the fragile
and fascinating species around us. She intends her essay collection to
work like a *Wunderkammer*, a cabinet of curiosities. Each essay captures
a wonder of the natural world, or of human beings' connection with it:
falcons and boars; nature guides and baby birds of prey; women who
feed badgers biscuits and raise baby swifts, an epidemiologist seeking
asylum. 'Literature can teach us the qualitative texture of the world,' she

writes. 'And we need it to. We need to communicate the value of things, so that more of us might fight to save them.'

Macdonald's love of nature began during her childhood. The essays take us to Tekels Park, the estate established by the Theosophical Society in Camberley. There, Macdonald searched for newts, grass snakes and birds, surrounded by people of 'luminous eccentricity' (one woman wore ancient Egyptian jewellery; another kept a great auk's egg in a drawer). After Tekels Park was sold to a property developer, Macdonald finds that her grieving for the lost butterflies that once lived there is tempered with the knowledge that the meadow lies dormant, as seeds deep in the soil, and might grow again one day.

Macdonald's passion for birds resonates throughout the collection. When a landlord pays an unwelcome visit, the son of the new prospective tenants is charmed by Macdonald's parrot: 'The boy just loves the bird... soon the bird and the boy are both swaying sideways, backwards and forwards, dancing at each other.' The writer delights in seeing black-crowned night herons amid the high rises of Manhattan, and peregrine falcons at a power station on the Irish coast. 'Swan Upping' looks at royal birds, British tradition, pageantry, and counter-narratives to nationalism. Macdonald searches for alternative ways of thinking about the annual ceremonial health-check and census of the monarch's swans. She celebrates the skilful handling and ringing of the birds, the practised manoeuvring of skiffs, and the way the painter Stanley Spencer, who painted the 'upping', travelled to China and found unexpected cultural links with Premier Zhou Enlai. A beautiful moment of connection between woman and swan occurs later in the collection, when the author meets one by a lock in Cambridge. 'I never cared much for swans until the day a swan told me I was wrong... a female mute swan hoist herself out from the water and stumped towards me on leathery, in-turned webbed feet and sturdy black legs.' The swan sits next to her by the river, pressing her wing-feathers against Macdonald's legs. This animal encounter is both humorous and moving:

I didn't know what to do: I grasped, bewildered, for the correct interspecies social etiquette. She looked at me incuriously, then tucked her head sideways and backwards into her raised coverts, neck curved, and fell fast asleep… a swan had come towards me and offered me strange companionship at a time when I thought loneliness was all I could feel.

The title essay, 'Vesper Flights', explores the evening ascent of swifts. This is not only so that the birds can sleep in the air (although during the First World War, a French aviator once caught two drowsing birds from his plane), but may also enable them to view oncoming weather systems and orient themselves. Such ascents also take place just before dawn. The wonder of flight ties together many of these pieces. 'Ants' is about the nuptial flight of common black ant, and it will help many readers to see this garden species with fresh eyes: an ant queen can live for thirty years; the queens take flight, chased by male drones, and will only mate with those who can fly the highest. Macdonald evokes 'a vault of sky crossed with thousands of different flightlines, warm airspace tense with predatory intent and the tiny hopes of each rising ant.' There is a humility, an antidote to human-centred thinking, when Macdonald acknowledges that 'I'm little more than an ant in the wider workings of the world, no more or less important than any of the creatures here.'

Her powers of description and defamiliarisation are keen. A drinker moth caterpillar is 'like a curiously mobile moustache'. Seeing a British wild boar, which looks 'nothing like a pig', the author reflects that 'It had the forward-menacing shoulders of a baboon and the brute strength and black hide of a bear.' There are also fascinating and moving animal encounters. The anecdotes about rearing falcons in Wales are delightful:

Every year we'd hand-rear a few falcons and raise them in the office. I'd find fledglings fast asleep on my keyboard, squeaking irritably and sending feather-dust into the air when I gently

nudged them awake and asked them to move so I could type.
Sometimes I'd roll scrunched-up paper balls to them across the
laminate floor and they'd run, stumpily, unsteadily, wings half-
open, grabbing at their rolling targets with feet that weren't yet
entirely coordinated, chittering with high excitement.

Macdonald admits that her childhood obsession with capturing animals
was ethically dubious: 'Rescuing animals made me feel good about
myself; surrounded by them I felt less alone.' And yet she realises that,
in later life, falconry taught her how to empathise with the falcon, to
anticipate its needs, to know exactly when it was fed up with training.
We anthropomorphise animals, she reflects, and yet being observed by
a rook in flight 'stitched me back into a world where both of us have
equal billing.'

Jasmine Donahaye's *Birdsplaining: A Natural History* also delights in birds
and animals, exploring field guides and the history of ornithology; hospital visits; memories of a sister who loved keeping finches; climbing
a sea cliff; looking for eagles; a polecat in the attic, and a parrot who
loves destroying computer keys. There are major themes here: mortality;
exploitation of the natural world; colonial dominance, and patriar-
chal oppression. The first essay, 'Reading the Signs', is a masterpiece of
memoir. It weaves together a narrative of birds and butterflies as por-
tents; the story of how she and her sister tried to keep budgies, finches
and quails; her sister's death from cancer before Donahaye had the
chance to say goodbye, and the trauma of an abusive relationship. The
author sees the autumn equinox, the anniversary of her sister's death,
as layered with signs: magpies; blood-red hawthorn berries; a scaveng-
ing kite, her own yearly hospital visits to check for cancer. The morning
before the phone call announcing the death came, an ominous event
occurred: a bird flew into her house, often considered to foretell a death
in the family. The author 'found a wren battering against the inside of

the bathroom window. I caught it, frantic and scrabbling, and I held it, and I took it outside, and I knew my sister was going to die.'

Donahaye writes of 'wind entering you, surrounding you, embracing and throwing you, like a man who lives with rage,' and such visceral images of male dominance run through the essay collection. *Birdsplaining* pokes fun at patronising male, middle-aged twitchers with their comically oversized scopes and lenses (Donahaye encounters one specimen in a pink pullover, who points out a corncrake even though everyone already knows what it is). 'Birdwatching has always been predominantly a male interest, and bird books are predominantly written and illustrated by men,' she observes. A 1974 bird guide is dedicated to the authors' 'long-suffering wives'. In such books, the male bird is depicted as 'upright' and 'bold,' and the female as 'demure' and 'submissive'. Some species are represented only by the male. This kind of attitude has wider consequences: 'By extension, it's no surprise, I suppose, that I find it difficult to see the equal value of my own life, or any woman's life, when viewed through such familiar and easily recognisable patterns,' Donahaye writes. Contemporary bird guides contain colour photos of both male and female birds. However, the language of hunting and sexual conquest persists in birdwatching circles. Even when he is treating fellow male, nerdy birders with humour, nature writer Mark Cocker discusses the voyeurism of birdwatching, quoting a man who sees a coveted rarity exclaiming, 'It were so good I nearly creamed me pants.' Donahaye also researches a Victorian gentleman naturalist, Henry Baker Tristram, who collected the skins of more than 20,000 birds in Palestine. (The Tristram's grackle is named after him.) His attitudes towards local people in Palestine reflected the imperialist racism of the time, although he depended on his helper Gemil, who possessed a deep understanding of the region's wildlife – and even saved Tristram's own life.

If Victorian naturalists were exclusively white and male, some rural areas of England and Wales still appear to be white-dominated. Donahaye criticises narrow-minded attitudes about locality and belonging that

DAWN CHORUS, VESPER FLIGHTS

prevail in such areas. She tells of racist slurs in the playground, anti-semitic hate-speech and constant questions from rural people about where she's 'from'. She is concerned that 'racism and green politics find themselves such easy bedfellows' in the work of authors such as Henry Williamson, who published *Tarka the Otter* and later joined the British Union of Fascists. Yet diverse voices in modern nature writing, from Jini Reddy to Mya-Rose Craig and indeed Donahaye herself, suggest that much-needed changes are afoot.

In many nature memoirs by women, the personal is already politi-cal, ecological, and wild. In her essay 'Mansplaining the Wild', Donahaye considers the reviewer Jim Hinch, who criticises women nature writers such as Cheryl Strayed for bringing the personal into their nature writing. Hinch finds such hybrid memoirs 'human-centred and inward looking', although the likes of Robert Macfarlane, whom Hinch terms a 'mountaineer and academic' and the current 'dean' of nature writing, are apparently more in tune with the 'natural world itself'. Yet there are plenty of women who are deeply 'in tune' in this collection. Donahaye's essays let us meet women who have a deep understanding of land and animal management, and who revel in adventurous pursuits. The author accompanies two women who cull and gralloch hinds on Skye, and tells us about a small girl in Palestine who assisted Tristram with raiding a griffon vulture's nest by clambering down a cliff on a rope. This is a beautiful collection where the nonhuman appears as a close neigh-bour: a sheep straying into the author's house, a solitary bee looking to make a home in her walls, a pet parrot chewing the author's binocu-lars or – more disturbingly – a flood seeping into the house. As it turns towards essays about illness and her sister's aversion to medical treat-ment, the collection searches for hope and resilience in times of risk.

Jay Griffiths' *Nemesis, My Friend* is arranged into four movements, 'Dawn'; 'Noon'; 'Evening', and 'Night'. It opens with creation myths and the Greek goddess Nemesis. Nemesis is not a frightening character who symbolises retribution but instead the goddess of boundaries and limits. In times of climate change, pandemic and political corruption, Griffiths invokes Nemesis to restore proper limits to people and planet. 'All is not right with the world,' Griffiths writes. 'We have blindly become arsonists. The climate is like a parasol or umbrella, protecting the world. Our generation has set fire to the very thing that was our defence.'

The first essay begins with the dawn chorus. 'It is dawn in the woods near my home. I come here most days because the birds, chissicking and fluting, enliven me, quicken me.' Birds and birdsong are woven throughout the collection; the final essay is 'Sacred Hospitality', which celebrates the way Griffiths' friend Jan stands a garden fork in the ground so that a robin can perch there. Griffiths is often praised for her poetic prose, and her descriptions of birdsong do not disappoint: 'the madrigal widens to a crescendo of coloratura as each bird becomes the maestro of its own cadenza into full morning.' Cellist Beatrice Harrison recorded her duets with nightingales; Keats and Shelley were moved to poetry by its song; and yet a silent spring is looming: Britain's nightingale population fell by 91% between 1967 and 2007. Griffiths' work finds moments of joy and sacredness in the everyday: she reflects on the Balinese custom of *canang sari* or everyday offerings.

Yet problems occur when people can't have their comforting rituals: all those postponed weddings and cancelled funerals during Covid. Griffiths uses a stark, hard-hitting style with great skill: 'My father died during lockdown. There was no funeral.' Her father's remembered presence is threaded through other essays in the book, including a picaresque 'visit' to Prague, a city that her father loved. Because she cannot actually travel during the pandemic, Griffiths sets off for an imaginary city break on the back of a friendly horse called Herbie. She 'encounters' flea circuses and flea markets. The essay draws on Angelo Ripellino's *Magic Prague*, written when the author could not travel to Prague during communism: in his book, places are categorised as 'existing', 'existing under a different name' or 'no longer existing'. Griffiths writes that her father would have loved the unlimited beer refills in the House of the Black Cat bar and enjoyed the sewage museum. In an absurd yet poignant way, she finds him: 'I know with absolute assurance that he is here, my father, turning the rudiments of actuality into humour, safely protected from the emotional content of art, taking an engineer's delight in what is both unexpected and explicable. I have found my father.'

There is playful celebration, too, in the essay 'Dawn: A Trouserful of Wantonness' [a version of which was years ago published in *New Welsh Review*]. Griffiths visits the grave of the much-loved (and lustful) fourteenth-century Welsh poet Dafydd ap Gwilym. She touches the old, lightning-ravaged yew under which he is buried:

> *When the lightning struck this yew, the fire that followed had, with uncanny precision, transformed the tree into the shape of a harp. I crawl through it, beneath its twisting striations of yew-wood like the curls of a treble clef, or the waves of smoke in the wind, to sit right inside, leaning back against the heart of the tree, all charcoal now. With that charcoal, I write in a page of my notebook, 'Thank you, Dafydd'.*

The encounter with his writing continues: 'Leaning forward, I realise that the charcoal has traced its black lettering lines over my coat. I've been written on.' A local harpist even has a piece of the tree embedded in her harp, for 'making music which resounds with him'. Griffiths and friends spend a rough night in the graveyard – Griffiths sleeping in the hollow yew itself during a storm. 'Dafydd lives, alive, thriving, green and invoked,' she reflects, when the harpist arrives in the morning and the wind makes the strings of the harp resound.

If some nature writers have a reputation for being straight-laced, Griffiths delights in humour and playfulness: children and puppies sliding about on a frozen lake in Wales, her kitten Otter dashing in 'curly crazy circles' after a toy mouse. One of her more political essays uses mischievous humour to mock English nationalist politicians. She invokes the figure of the Trickster, that mythical animal or person who pokes fun at the powerful, likening Boris Johnson to Peppa Pig and calling Nigel Farage 'the drinking man's twat'.

Griffiths travels widely in these essays, and encounters ways of life that suggest welcome alternatives to the forms of bigotry and ethnic nationalism that characterise the thinking of Farage, Johnson and Trump. When visiting Indigenous cultural centres in Mexico, Griffiths reflects that 'Love for land is absolutely not the same as nationalism or blood-lines. Through humility, through humanity, through humus, Earth itself speaks to the indigenous human mind.' She meets Indigenous educators in Mexico and environmental justice activists in West Papua, where torture and ethnic cleansing by the military are going largely unnoticed in the western media (the name of a friend of hers even appears on a hit list). She meets West Papuan activists who stand up against a genocidal military and multinational mining companies. "We are being killed for this thing called progress," said one Papuan man to me, bluntly.' Yet Griffiths celebrates their peaceful forms of protest: music and song.

Seeing wild animals is yet more precious when one realises how threatened they are. As Griffiths writes, 'If we humans are making other creatures cruelly homeless, the only answer is a politics of kindness, a chivalric devotion to the earth, and an honouring of the most ancient laws of sacred hospitality that extends to everything: a slate for the lichen, a home-scar for a limpet, a sett for a badger, a form for a hare, an eyrie for an eagle, a nest for a house marten, a roost for a bat – and a fork for a robin.'

Yvonne Reddick's books include *Ted Hughes: Environmentalist and Ecopoet* (Palgrave, 2017) and *Burning Season* (Bloodaxe, May 2023). Her work appears in *The Guardian* (Review) and the *New Statesman*.

Titles Under Discussion
Vesper Flights, Helen Macdonald (Vintage, 2021)
Birdsplaining: A Natural History, Jasmine Donahaye (New Welsh Rarebyte, 2023)
Nemesis, My Friend, Jay Griffiths (Little Toller, 2022)

New Welsh Review editor Gwen Davies is interviewing Jasmine Donahaye, Jay Griffiths and Rachel Hewitt in a session on Women and Nature at Hay Festival on 31 May (4pm, The Hive).

THANK YOU TO OUR #SECURENEWWELSHREVIEW SUPPORTERS

Diamond Supporters:
Mary Chadwick
Professor Tony Curtis
Mary Oliver
Kaite O'Reilly

Platinum Supporters:
Tasha Alden
Ruhi Behi
E Clifford Cutler
Jasmine Donahaye
Elaine Ewart
Katie Gramich

Kurt Heinzelman
Gareth Lewis
Rhiannon Lewis
Susan Merriman
Jackie Morris
Dr Chris W Pitt
Jim Pratt
Tracey Rhys
Amy Strange
Clive Upton
Roger Williams
Carole Hailey

AN EDEN

STORY BY **SIMON HOWELLS**

THE GRASS IS TOUGH AND YELLOW BUT THE SHEEP LIKE IT AND IT MUST BE good for them because their poo is black and shiny. The first time we went I thought it was rabbit poo and Sienna said *Big fucking rabbits*. There's a pond where they put fish. Sometimes quiet men sit with rods. The second time she said *It's the camels first* and I looked but couldn't see any and she nearly wet herself laughing. She was crying and saying she couldn't breathe and I wanted to join in but didn't have the laughter so I just smiled till she stopped. Then she told me to look back and I saw the hills. The humps.

We carried on. My head was hot and I worried I was starting a headache. I knew not to mention this. She would sneer. My mum had given me a bag of sweets but Sienna had taken control. *Good children always share* she said. Sienna said she was sweating under her tits and she shoved her hand up her t-shirt and billowed it. I blushed. She tickled me under the chin. The ground is dark and boggy in parts. Bubbly water came up round our shoes, our feet sank. There are planks for getting across. Sienna wobbled as she tiptoed. She pretended to lose her balance. She did it more when I laughed.

We settled on a rock to eat sweets. Wedding rings, fried eggs, snakes, pink hearts. Jellies. She was gazing across the water. I was wondering what was on her mind when she stood up and took off her t-shirt. I looked away but too late. Like googly eyes and moving by themselves. When I heard the splash I turned round. Water closed over her. Her t-shirt, skirt and shoes were in a line on the ground which made me sad for some reason.

Her head bobbed up darker now. Water slid down her face. She shouted *Jump in Gabe.* I said I didn't want to. Her bottom flashed as she went under again. I walked to the water's edge, searched the surface. I began counting. After ten seconds I felt sick. I laid the sweets down. When my t-shirt was round my ears my ankle was grabbed. I kicked out. There was no noise. My t-shirt off I yelled at her and she slipped beneath the water. I stepped out of my shorts and pants and thinking *If Mum could see me now* jumped in.

She swam to me and said *Well done Gabe.* Then she ducked me. I was angry but soon pleased. Part of something. Ducked her. Her head was greasy. A fish touched my leg and I screamed. Sienna laughed, I ran out of scream. She wrapped her arms round me and I started falling. I was lurching in my head. After she let go I returned to myself. I wished she would do it again and my wish was granted only this time she put her legs round me too and her hair tickled my stomach and the falling came on once more. She released but hung on to me and her face dead serious she said for us to go underwater. When I asked why she said *Just do it.*

We resurfaced and she said *Has he gone* and I said *Who* and she said *The man* and I said *What man* and she said there'd been a man watching us. She looked round. I didn't believe her. We were treading water. She swam to the side, pulled herself out. The knobbly line of her spine. Then she was holding her clothes in front of her. Shivering. When I climbed out she said *Look at his little man.*

My t-shirt and pants stuck to my skin but soaked water up and then the sun was shining so hard my hair was nearly dry. She was patting herself. I stepped into my shoes and wriggled my toes. I could tell the shape of her through her t-shirt. We walked, Sienna wondering if she had imagined the man. I said *It happens.* She was quiet. Then, stopping, she spoke. *Isn't it funny how we have words for things that aren't.* I said I didn't understand. *Like 'gap' and 'space' – and 'sky'.* She looked up. *It would* be great *if just for a minute all the things that aren't were, and they pushed themselves forward and bulged and everything else – cars and houses and supermarkets and trees and mountains and people – and everything else just went. Just for a minute.* She stayed still as if giving someone the chance to make this happen. Nothing happened and we moved on, ate more sweets.

Small, pale green, and so dry-looking I thought it was dead. *No – sunbathing* said Sienna. And when she nudged it with her shoe the snake curled the opposite way. I said *Be careful* and she snorted. I wanted to turn and run. I don't like snakes. The diamond pattern was faint on account of the dryness. *Hit it* said Sienna and took off her shoe to hand to me. *Hit it and I'll pick it up.* I said *It might bite you* and she said she would drop it in the sweet bag. We faced each other with the same idea. We are from the same family after all. A snake to go with the other snakes – and the wedding rings and fried eggs and pink hearts! *Have one* we'd say. Good children always share. *Yes* she said her eyes bright. *Let's do it. I don't want to* I said. I was full of dread. *Do it* she said. Her fingers curled round me. She owned me. I slashed the air. A trial run. Changed my grip, slashed again, faster this time. My stomach tensed. My head thumped. *Maybe I shouldn't have gone in the water. Maybe I've swallowed fish eggs.*

Hurry she said, *it might escape.*

The snake lifted its head and hissed. Bright black eyes. *I can't* I said. *Poof!* she said and I raised my arm and brought the shoe down. *Do it again* she said hopping. *Yes, again, again.* The snake wriggled this way and that with slime coming out of its head. *Don't stop* she said and closing my eyes I continued till exhausted. Then I opened my eyes. The body was shrivelled and drier-looking than before and the head flat and covered in brown ooze. I felt terrible. I had done a terrible thing. I started to cry.

It doesn't look like anything now said Sienna. *Not like a pretend snake. Not like a snake, even.* She took the shoe, sniffed it. *There's stuff on it.* She put her shoe back on. I was still crying. My sobs sounded far away.

What have you done. A tall man with a black beard and green sunhat.

The man. He picked the snake up. *What have you done* he repeated and Sienna said *We found it like this* and he said *Rubbish, I saw you. You were holding something. Something dark.* He looked round for the dark thing and I couldn't stop my eyes from wandering over to Sienna's feet. *Give me your shoes* he said and with a sneer she said *I saw you. You watched us in the water. You watched us for a long time. For too long.* And with that she turned and raced off. And I finally got my chance to run. But not before I had clocked the look on the man's face. A look of not-understanding.

Simon Howells was born in south Wales in 1971.

THE SUMMER OF NADIA COMĂNECI

Across the unkempt quarter acre a seven-year-old cartwheels a diagonal, reaches the last inches of grass before the sidewalk, and hops to a taut stance facing the direction she came, feet together, head high. She remembers to smile, though as far as she knows the dandelions are her only audience, before she repeats the run. Later, she'll walk the street's stone curb as though it were a balance beam, practise handstands against her bedroom wall. She'll linger at the magazine photo taped to the door: Nadia poised in the floor exercise, one knee cocked forward, arm angled with fingers splayed, and her smile, her radiant smile. One morning, coming in for a cold drink, she found her mother and her mother's friend talking in the dining room, and when the mother remarked on what her daughter had been doing, out there in the yard, the friend said, 'You do look a bit like her, that Nadia girl.' Oh, the girl knew. She knew how she felt executing a succession of mere cartwheels or balancing with a raised foot gracefully pointed. One day she'd smile, she'd smile like Nadia, and she wouldn't need anyone.

Carrie Etter's fourth and current poety collection is *The Weather in Normal* (Seren, 2018), while her fifth collection, *Grief's Alphabet*, will be published by Seren in 2024. She is a member of the creative writing faculty at the University of Bristol.

OUTWARD BOUND

That weekend in the Brecon Beacons: twenty
adolescents out for some team building,
abseiling, caving, endless afternoons
of wandering through fields of buttercups

or sheepshit. All of us the age we were:
the girls who took to hanging round the boys' dorm,
all trampolining curls and brand-new sports kit,
until the teachers made some bones about it,

the two who hung back at the nature ramble
and re-emerged all grins, excuses, grass stains,
the boy at midnight knocking the girls' window
who swore on his mother's life he'd been sleepwalking,

or him whose kayak tipped in the white water
and kept up the illusion that he'd drowned
long enough for some fulsome mouth-to-mouth.
Me, it was my first time that far from home
and I just hoped that I could get back safely,

but still, there was that one moment in the caves
when we all agreed to turn off our helmet lights,
so we could see what true darkness would be like,

and then, as that underground wind whistled round us,
I felt her take my dangling right hand in hers
and whisper the first syllable of my name

and suddenly, right then and there, I was thirteen,
knowing for sure that I could see nothing in this world
and that I'd never know where the hell I was,

ever again.

ARROWS

He is a man for whom his eye, his wrist
and the relationship of that to this,
the distance between here and there, the six
feet from him to board or the half inch
of throw to thought is all there is. He is

a man with a regime, a tight routine
of practice, pies and pints, a nickname sewn
or sequinned here across his shirt, his back,
whose wrist, whose throat just dangles, drips with gold,
a waist-slashed shirt his chest hair peeps or pokes

over. He's a man with all the numbers
there inside his head, can reel right off
his seventeen times table without blinking,
plot the smoothest route from 143
to double top, and when he sweats he sweats

Carling. He's a man who has his own
trophy cabinet, a singalong
theme tune, grown men who rhyme his name
ingeniously, he'll step up now and take
a decade's wages for a working man

between his thumb and finger, breathe in, glance
and let them go. A room full of applause
and what he thinks of are his nights alone
out in the garage, all the world asleep,
the music of a dart, a dart, a dart

hitting the board.

DAYS OF 1998

It started oh where did it start it started
in bedrooms blasting out the radio's
squalled guitars, its livid drums, its so-called
singing. Started with a screwball study
of all your favourite albums' liner'd lyrics'
reference to Sartre, Neruda, Kant,
your certainty that a guitar would bring you
everything that mattered. Sputtered, started

where it started: with a chat, a talk
outside a classroom, in a corridor
or over a shared smoke on sofas, floors
of rented flats or uni halls. A poster
you whacked up in a music shop might conjure
the very man to step out of the ether
and be the missing part of you or hey,
at least a halfway decent bassist, drummer

and then it really started. Where it started
was in a parents' shed you got kicked out of,
in after-hours music rooms of schools,
church halls you rented by the hour, promised,
pleaded to pay later. How it started
was with some gig, some Battle of the Bands,
or someone knew a bloke who knew a bloke
who owned the Mason's Arms. And when it started

it didn't stop: it lurched towards a future
of gold discs, vintage leather jackets, chronic
drug habits, premature death. Or else,
more like, there was a year or two of sleeping
in rusted Transits, waking up in Sheffield,
Norwich, Leeds, with everything you needed:
a thick head and a song to sing and there,
some fifty folk to hear it. There are lives

I never lived. In this one, one of us
is a computer programmer in Magor,
one works in Caffè Nero, one's a lawyer
and one of us (so says the internet)
has stuck with it, and plays around the clubs
of Malta, and he's loving it. The last
of us? He's sitting down. He's taking up
a pen and paper and he's starting now.

Jonathan Edwards' prize-winning poetry collections are *My Family and Other Superheroes* (Seren, 2014) and *Gen* (Seren, 2018). He received the Troubadour Poetry Prize in 2022, and lives in Crosskeys, Gwent.

I AM UNLEARNING

As a child, I always liked it the most
when I sat at the centre of the seesaw;
there, you didn't need to pick a side,
yet somehow, you still got the thrill

of the aching highs and the sudden lows.
I also found it was best to be agnostic
about where I preferred to spend Christmas.
My recurrent nightmare was that my parents

were drowning in a river and I had to choose
one of them to swim out to and save.
So, you'll forgive me if I find it difficult
to say what I'd like for dinner, or if I take

an hour deciding on a film to watch.
Choice is hard for some of us. And anyway,
perhaps my parents were fine in the river,
perhaps it was just my job to stay dry.

LET'S PRETEND

On her death bed, my grandma hallucinated
I was standing beside her, aged about five,
my mouth wide open. She told my mum:
Tell Julia to shut her mouth or she'll catch flies.

I don't doubt that little me was present
dressed in nurse's fancy dress,
toy stethoscope around my neck,
placing a plastic disc on her papery chest,

setting a fake thermometer between her false teeth,
scrawling the self-important observations of a child
– heart rate, temperature, pulse – arranging
a well-meaning vase of cheap pink carnations.

So awed was I by the atrophy of her body
I allowed my jaw to drop for a second;
after decades of pretence I wanted,
just once, for her to see who I really was.

Julia Forster received a Society of Authors grant in 2022 for her first poetry collection, currently in development. As an undergraduate at Warwick, she was awarded the Derek Walcott Prize for poetry and went on to study for an MLitt in Creative Writing at St Andrews University. Her nonfiction book, *Muses: Revealing the Nature of Inspiration*, was published by Oldcastle Books in 2007, while her debut novel, *What a Way to Go* was published in 2016 by Atlantic. Her poems have been published in anthologies and magazines, including *As Above So Below* (ed Bethany Rivers), *Poetry Wales, Hiraeth / Erzolirzoli* (ed Eric Ngalle Charles), *Poems from Snowdonia* (ed Amy Wack) and *The Result is What you See Today* (eds Kim Moore, Paul Deaton & Ben Wilkinson). In 2020, she won the Lockdown Poetry Prize in *The Telegraph*, and last year her poem, 'Invisible Sisterhood', had a top ten honorary mention in the Fish Poetry Prize and was published in the *Fish Poetry Anthology*. writewithin.wales

BOULEVARD SAINT-LAURENT

Alys Robi on the steps of Le National. 'La Main, c'était une époque.' Late beers at Le Swimming, cue-clicks softened by low-lit green baize. The slack rhythm of taxi tyres on salt roads. Writing letters home in The Shed over pancakes, riffing on the clutch of the cold. But the sky is a crackling blue in the morning, amaranthine late afternoon. I think of le fleuve, ice shifting and fixing, canoes and pine. There's a double time feel, violet light. Elle's parked up somewhere, likely ran into Schwartz's if the line's not too long. The tang of the pickles just right for this night which freezes your breath in your nose. Will's chewing gum at la Cabane. I'm dancing with strangers in La Sala Rossa, stomping to sea shanties. Or grooving to afrobeat at Casa del Popolo: 'Lady''s my favourite song. It's -20 outside, but I'm in a vest top, shirt round my waist, whole-tone. A laughing kiss, a lipstick kiss, a brief touch of tongues. In a studio on Mentana, I trace 'still' on his chest, gape at shoulders shaped by hours in the pool. Pause, then resume: grammar, vocabulary, structure and form. Oscar Peterson plays, ride cymbal tagging along. It's late, traffic's thin, cars but occasional commas in the endless story of the city with ink in the veins, on the skin. 'Il fait si noir. Tellement de choses peuvent arriver à notre corps.' My measured hope. Fy nghariad, je t'aimerai toujours. Tomorrow, we'll walk by Leonard Cohen's house, listen to 'Suzanne'. Go to Laïka for coffee. Always.

WORD WOUND

~~Word~~. ~~Wound~~. 'The strike scars and lasts'. A skewed preposition. A scratch on skin. My clothes cut away and my abdomen flipped open. She told me something unhearable. Blackout, trou de mémoire, a memory hole into which I fell and fell. I put a pebble in the place of my heart. Retraction. Repetition. My accent stitched up my tongue. There were times when I slipped: a girl climbing out of my adult body, unzipping my stomach to stand, rigid with fear. Midline shift. Pulled off-centre. A danger of death. A brief tussle and the bottom half of my baby thrust for a second over the screen. The white noise of morphine. 'Falling out of love'. Cariad. Recoil. Re-wind/~~-wound~~. A flash of violet. I tried to write the pain, but I was just too damn happy.

Notes

['Boulevard…', 'La Main, c'était une époque'] Nicole Brossard, French Kiss (Montréal: Quinze, 1980 [Éditions du Jour, 1974]).

['Boulevard…', 'Il fait si noir….'] Brossard, *French Kiss*.

[Boulevard] Cited with the kind permission of Nicole Brossard.

['Word Wound', 'The strike scars and lasts'] Jacob Marie-Andrée and Anna Macdonald, 'A Change of Heart: Retraction and Body', *Law Text Culture* (2019), https://ro.uow.edu.au/ltc/vol23/iss1/15. Cited with the kind permission of Marie-Andrée Jacob and Anna Macdonald.

['Word Wound', 'Falling out of love'] Jacob and Macdonald.

Ceri Morgan is from Hirwaun but spent most of her adult life working on Québec fiction. French has become her second language, but she has retained some Welsh, which she studied as an acquired language for A level. She has also retained a strong Valleys accent in English. 'Boulevard Saint-Laurent' is the fourth in a series of poems about Montréal, which punctuates an ongoing creative nonfiction memoir. Set in different seasons and in various neighbourhoods, these play with the layering of cultures and histories in and of the city, time, mobility, gender, desire and language.

VERY CLEAR AND DETAILED IN THE ODD BRILLIANT LIGHT

very clear and detailed in the odd brilliant light
— Iris Murdoch

on the sideboard   your favourite cup   a memory of tea leaves very
     faint   settled into contours of painted violets   clear
     though clarity was never the point   ga'i de   you said and
     llâth   so we boiled the kettle again   detailed
     our histories   sipped   sunk like whiskey   redrawn in
     reflections of your hair   the silver through your breath   the
     chain you gave me   twenty-one   you thought it odd
I couldn't accept   until   bydda i'n anghofio   you said   so brilliant
against the fire   paid byth anghofio fy mod yn dy garu di   my light

Elizabeth Chadwick-Pywell is an English/Welsh poet living in York, whose latest pamphlet, *Breaking (Out)*, was published by Selcouth Station; her first, *Unknown*, is available from Stairwell Books. She has featured in journals, including *Fourteen Poems* and *Dreich*, and in 2022 was longlisted for the Leeds Poetry Prize, shortlisted for the Ironbridge Festival Prize, and won the Northern Writer's Debut Award for Poetry.